EVERYBODY'S UKULELE METHOD

A STEP-BY-STEP APPROACH

"Ukulele Mike" Lynch, Philip Groeber

CONTENTS

Production: Frank Hackinson

Production Coordinator: Philip Groeber

Cover Design: Terpstra Design, San Francisco

"Ukulele Mike" Logo Design: Mike Hind

Engraving: Tempo Music Press, Inc.

Printer: Tempo Music Press, Inc.

Recordings by: "Ukulele Mike" at Robert Lang Studios, Seattle, WA

Engineer: Chris Rahm

Ukulele featured on cover: Oscar Schmidt "Ukulele Mike" model
courtesy of U.S. Music Corp.

THE
F·J·H
MUSIC
COMPANY
INC.
Frank J. Hackinson

ISBN-13: 978-1-61928-016-8

THE UKULELE

Parts of the ukulele

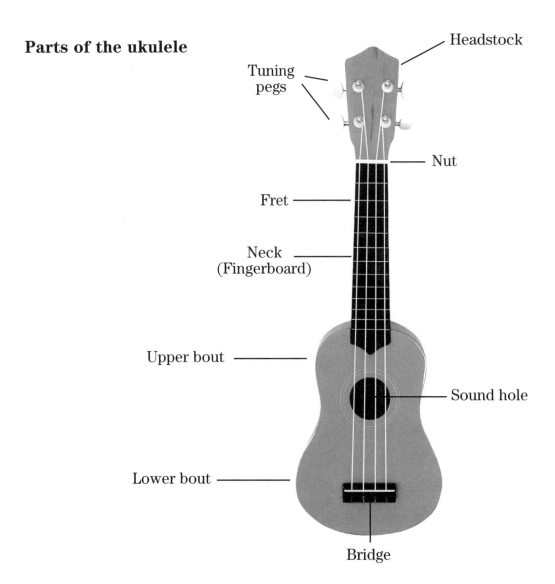

- Headstock
- Tuning pegs
- Nut
- Fret
- Neck (Fingerboard)
- Upper bout
- Sound hole
- Lower bout
- Bridge

Different types of ukuleles

Below is a chart showing the 4 types of ukuleles with their approximate height and number of frets. The most common size ukulele for beginners is the soprano. More advanced players prefer a ukulele with more frets. The largest ukulele, the baritone, sounds more like a guitar and is tuned DGBE, like the first four strings of a guitar.

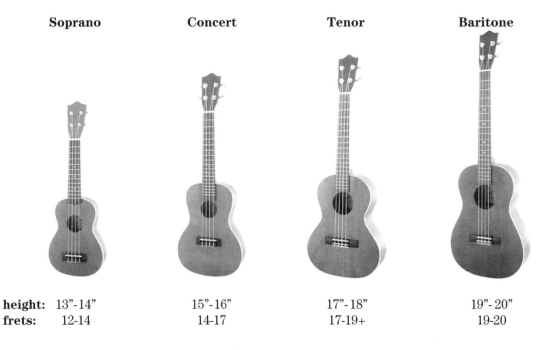

	Soprano	Concert	Tenor	Baritone
height:	13"–14"	15"–16"	17"–18"	19"–20"
frets:	12-14	14-17	17-19+	19-20

G1049

HOW TO PLAY THE UKULELE

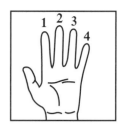

Left-Hand Technique
Ukulele Mike says, "Press the string down directly behind the fret, *not* on top
of it. Keep your wrist relaxed, do not grip the neck like a baseball bat!"
The left-hand fingers are numbered 1, 2, 3, 4.

Right-Hand Technique
Use the side of your thumb to strum down (toward the floor) when playing notes. See pages
30 and 47 for right-hand technique when strumming chords. A pick may be used.

Posture
Standing - Cradle the ukulele with your right arm. Strum downward with your thumb at the point
where the neck of the ukulele meets the body, not over the sound hole. Hold the ukulele high
on your body. This allows you to partly hold the uke up in the crook of your elbow. It also helps
you to hear the ukulele if you are singing, since it is closer to your ears. Your right forearm
should point right up the uke's neck. Generally the ukulele is held pressed tightly against the
body with the right arm, but a ukulele strap can help you keep your uke in place, especially
in the case of a tenor or baritone ukulele.

To attach a strap you will need to have a strap button attached to the end of the body of the
ukulele. It is best to have a trained technician do this for you. Have another button attached to
the heel of the neck on the underside where it meets the body of the uke. Others might like to
tie it off up above the nut on the headstock with a nylon or leather cord. The ukulele "thong"
strap is favored by many people as well and doesn't require the installation of a strap button.

Sitting - The lower bout of the ukulele should rest against your right thigh. Your right arm
keeps the uke snug against your body. A ukulele strap can be helpful here also.

Standing

Sitting

Tablature
In addition to the five-line staff of music, we also include
tablature in this book. Tablature (TAB) for the ukulele is a
four-line staff, with each horizontal line representing a string
of the ukulele. When holding the ukulele in playing position,
the string closest to the floor is the first string. The numbers
on the lines tell you which fret to play with your left hand;
that's it! *Tablature makes playing the ukulele fun and easy.*

Terms in **boldface** throughout the book are important concepts for you to know and
understand. Research these terms to further expand your general knowledge of music.

MUSIC FUNDAMENTALS

THE STAFF

Music is written on the **staff**, which has five lines and four spaces.

THE TREBLE CLEF

The **treble** (or **G**) **clef** is placed at the beginning (left side) of each staff of ukulele music.

LINE NOTES

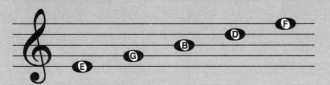

Each **line** has a letter name:

Every **G**ood **B**oy **D**oes **F**ine

SPACE NOTES

Each **space** has a letter name:

F   A   C   E

PITCH

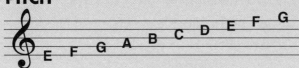

Pitch is the highness or lowness of a music tone. The higher the pitch, the higher a note is placed on the staff. The lower the pitch, the lower a note is placed on the staff. The names of notes come from the music alphabet A–G.

RHYTHM VALUES

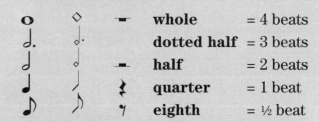

notes	strums	rests		
𝅝	◇	▬	whole	= 4 beats
𝅗𝅥.	◇.	▬.	dotted half	= 3 beats
𝅗𝅥	◇	▬	half	= 2 beats
♩	◇	𝄾	quarter	= 1 beat
♪	♪	𝄿	eighth	= ½ beat

Note values (𝅝 𝅗𝅥. 𝅗𝅥 ♩ ♪) indicate the duration of each pitch. Each musical note indicates both the pitch to be played *and* how long to let the tone sound.

BAR LINES AND MEASURES

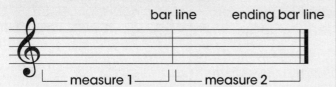

Bar lines divide the staff into equal parts called **measures**. An **ending bar line** is used to show the end of a piece of music.

THE TIME SIGNATURE

The $\frac{4}{4}$ (four-four) **time signature** tells us:

4 = four beats per measure
4 = the quarter note (♩) gets one beat

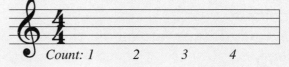

Count: 1   2   3   4

G1049

TUNING THE UKULELE

It is very important that your ukulele be tuned correctly each time you practice.

1. Electronic tuner

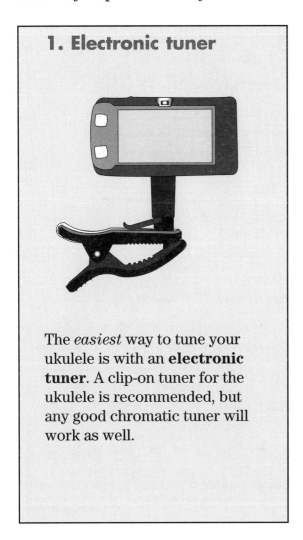

The *easiest* way to tune your ukulele is with an **electronic tuner**. A clip-on tuner for the ukulele is recommended, but any good chromatic tuner will work as well.

2. Piano keyboard

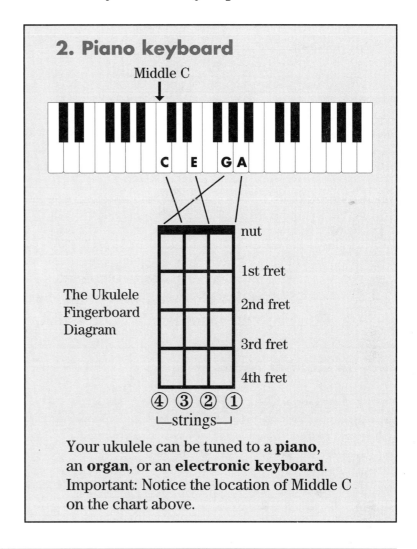

The Ukulele Fingerboard Diagram

Your ukulele can be tuned to a **piano**, an **organ**, or an **electronic keyboard**. Important: Notice the location of Middle C on the chart above.

3. Tuning the ukulele to itself (relative tuning)

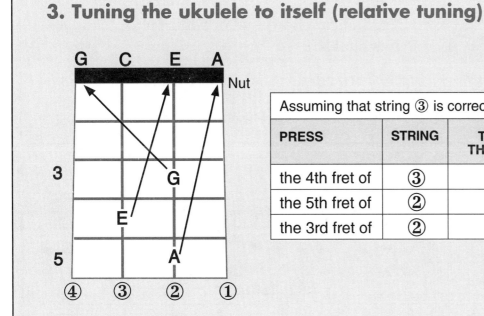

Assuming that string ③ is correctly tuned to C:			
PRESS	**STRING**	**TO GET THE PITCH**	**TO TUNE OPEN STRING**
the 4th fret of	③	**E**	②
the 5th fret of	②	**A**	①
the 3rd fret of	②	**G**	④

TRACK
1 Introduction

TRACK
2 Tuning notes: G C E A

NOTES ON THE THIRD STRING

C

open
string

D

2nd fret
2nd finger

QUARTER NOTES

The **quarter note** gets one beat. ♩ = 1 beat
Strum down (⊓) with your thumb to play *Study in Quarter Notes*.
Play and count evenly, with a steady beat.

or

← stem

← notehead

Study in Quarter Notes

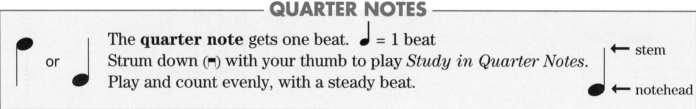

The line going through the notehead C is called a **ledger line**.

DYNAMICS

Dynamics are symbols and words that indicate how loud or soft to play.
The following symbols are used in this book:

p = *piano* (soft)   *mf* = *mezzo forte* (medium loud)   *f* = *forte* (loud)

If the music has no dynamic level indicated, play *mf* (medium loud).

Different Levels

③

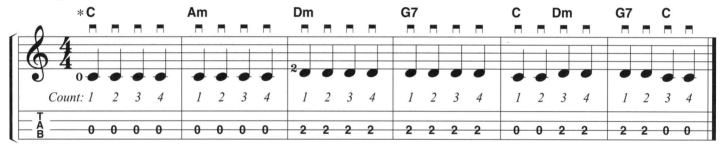

* The symbols above the staff (C, Am, G7, etc.) are chord names. If you would like to learn to strum chords at this time, go to page 30.

G1049

HALF NOTES

The **half note** gets two beats. ♩ = 2 beats
Be sure to let the half note ring for two full beats.

Study in Half Notes

**Circle the measures that contain an incorrect number of beats.
Look at the top number of the time signature to help you.**

④

The Jumping Flea

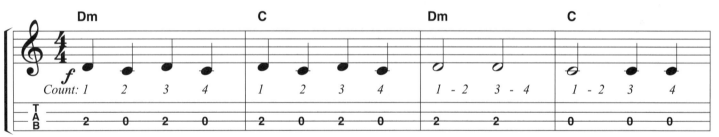

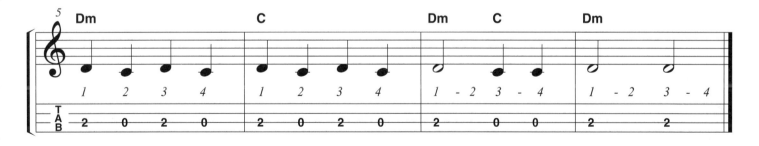

Many people think of Hawaii when they see or hear a ukulele. A rough translation of the word ukulele, is "jumping flea," pertaining to the actions of the hands as they play. But the former queen (and composer) of Hawaii, Queen Lili'uokalani (1838–1917), writes that the name means "the gift that came here."

NOTES ON THE SECOND STRING

E — open string

F — 1st fret, 1st finger

G — 3rd fret, 3rd finger

Study on the Second String

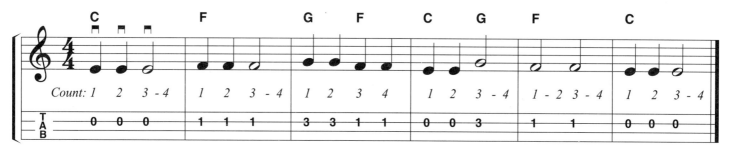

STRING CROSSING

String crossing is a term used when the notes move from one string to another.
With practice your right-hand thumb will easily learn this motion. Play as smoothly as possible.

Ukulele Mike Sez:
"Keep your fingers nicely arched over the strings. Your wrist should be relaxed".

Are You Sleeping?
Traditional French Round

Play several times without stopping

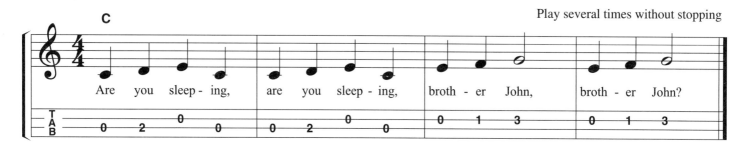

Are you sleep - ing, are you sleep - ing, broth - er John, broth - er John?

Follow the indicated fingering for the left hand carefully to establish good playing habits. Keeping your fingerboard fingers spread out will help you play the notes smoothly and with a rich, full sound.

G1049

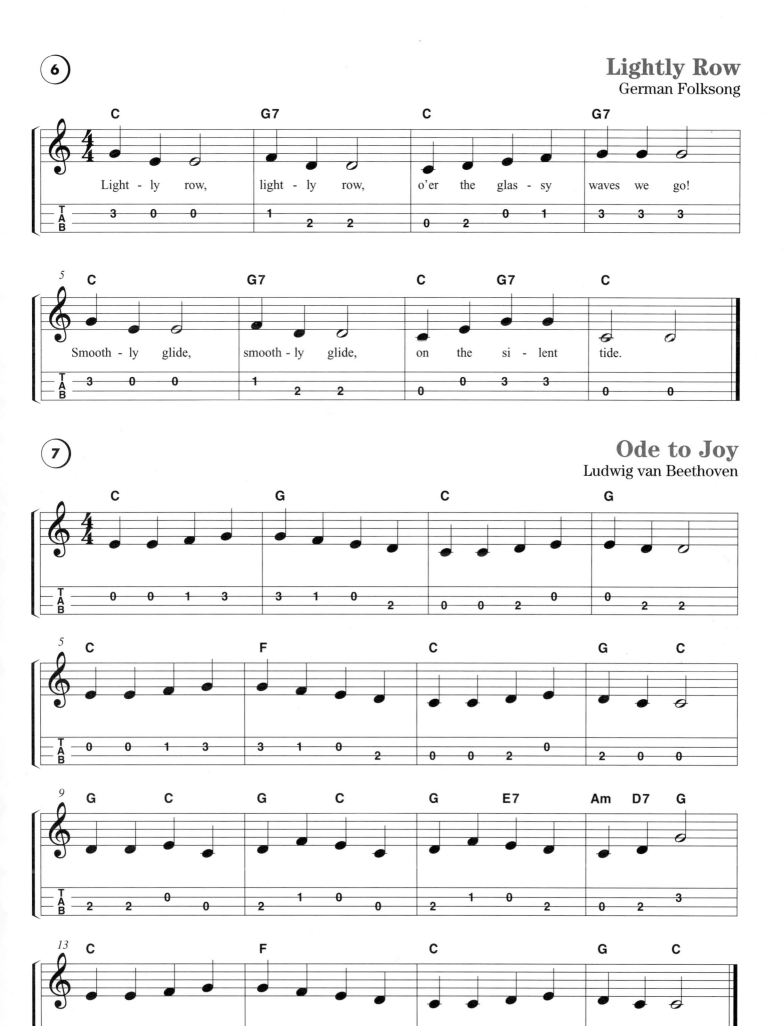

Lightly Row
German Folksong

Ode to Joy
Ludwig van Beethoven

The rhythm in measures 4, 8, and 16 may be learned by rote. ♩. ♪♩

NOTES ON THE FIRST STRING

A

open
string

B

2nd fret
2nd finger

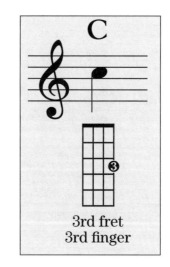

C

3rd fret
3rd finger

Study on the First String

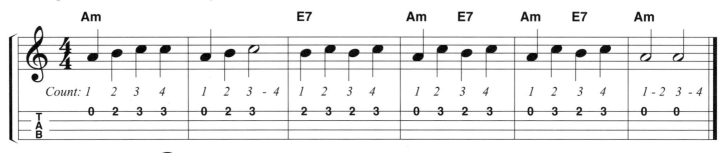

By the Sea (8)

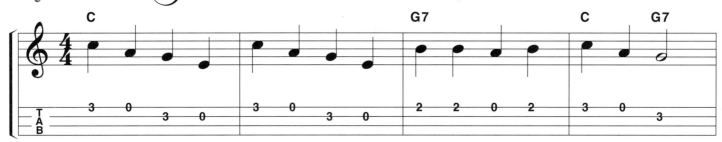

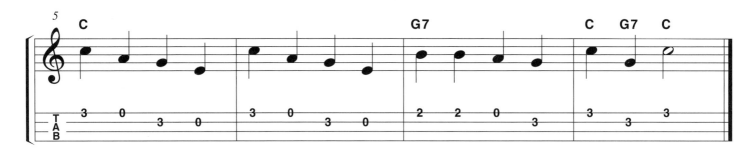

Write in the TAB numbers for the following melody. Then play.

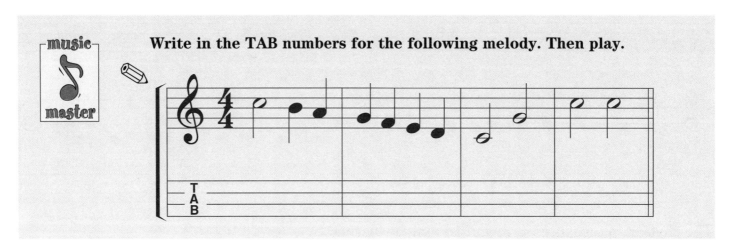

10

WHOLE NOTES

𝗼 The whole note gets four beats. 𝗼 = 4 beats
Four even counts must take place before you play the next note.
Count "1-2-3-4" for each whole note. **Always keep an even, steady beat.**

Study in Whole Notes

Holding a whole note for four counts is a very important element of rhythm. Small quarter notes are included above to remind you that whole notes receive four full counts.

THE KEY OF C MAJOR

Below is a chart of all of the notes you have learned so far. Notice that when consecutive notes are in alphabetical order, the notes will alternate either being line or space notes. These notes are the exact notes that make up a **C major scale**. Scales comprise the building blocks for melody in almost all of the music we hear. Songs that use the notes in the C scale are said to be in the **Key of C**. The first and last chords of the song will probably be C.

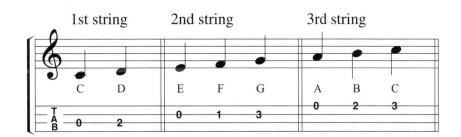

Memorize the C major scale below, and practice it every day for one minute (or longer).

⑨

The C major scale, ascending and descending   Play several times

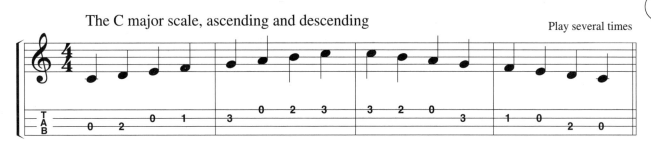

¾ TIME SIGNATURE

Music with a ¾ **time signature** gets three beats per measure. Each beat is equal to one quarter note.

DOTTED HALF NOTES

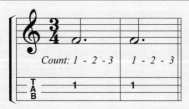

A dot placed after a note increases the value of the note by one half of its value. The **dotted half note** gets *three* beats.

♩ (2 beats) + ♩ (1 beat) = ♩. (3 beats)

Rhythm Study in ¾ Time *(Be sure you are counting three beats in a measure!)*

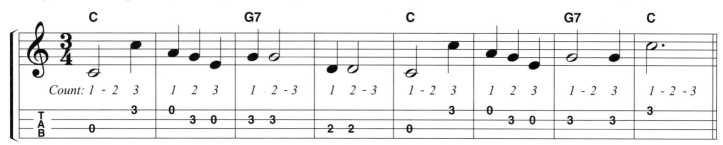

Sail Away ⑩

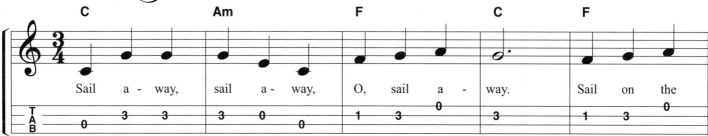

Count: 1 - 2 - 3

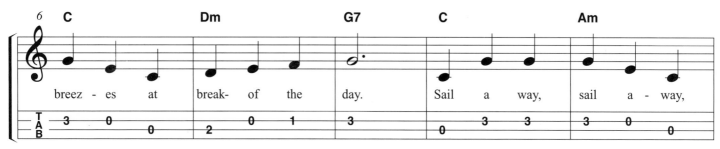

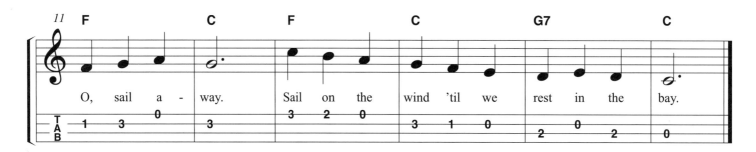

12

G1049

Beautiful Brown Eyes
Traditional

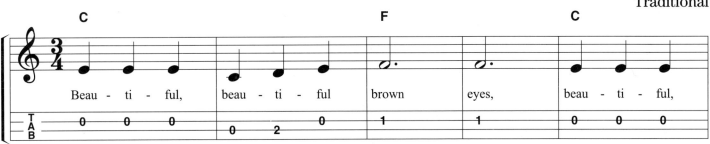

Beau - ti - ful, beau - ti - ful brown eyes, beau - ti - ful,

Count: 1 - 2 - 3   1 - 2 - 3

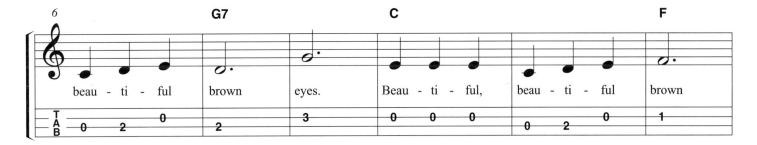

beau - ti - ful brown eyes. Beau - ti - ful, beau - ti - ful brown

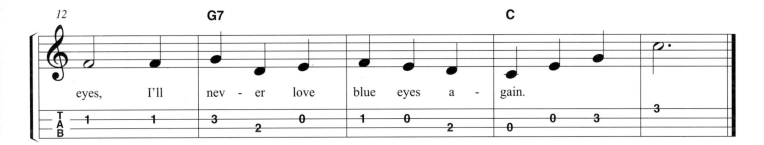

eyes, I'll nev - er love blue eyes a - gain.

Pop! Goes the Weasel!
Traditional

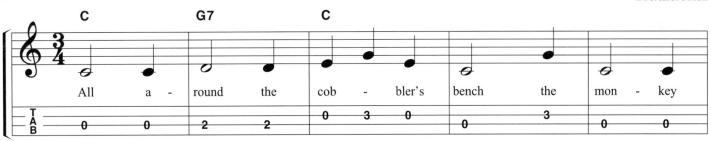

All a - round the cob - bler's bench the mon - key

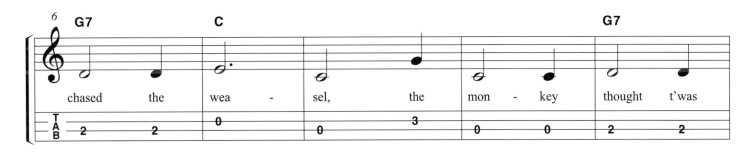

chased the wea - sel, the mon - key thought t'was

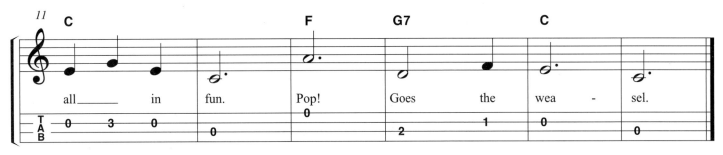

all___ in fun. Pop! Goes the wea - sel.

Pick-up notes are notes that come before the first complete measure. The beats in the pick-up measure and the last measure usually add up to one complete measure.

For He's a Jolly Good Fellow ⑬
Traditional Folksong

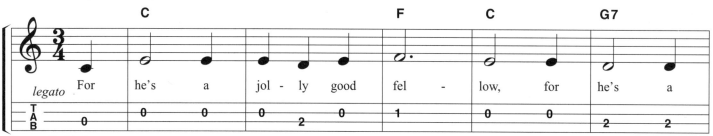

legato For he's a jol - ly good fel - low, for he's a

Count: (1 2) 3

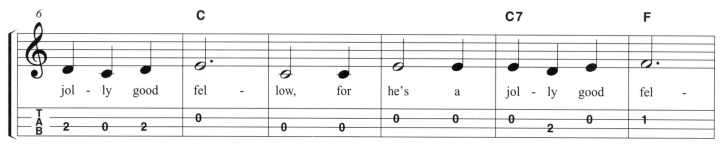

jol - ly good fel - low, for he's a jol - ly good fel -

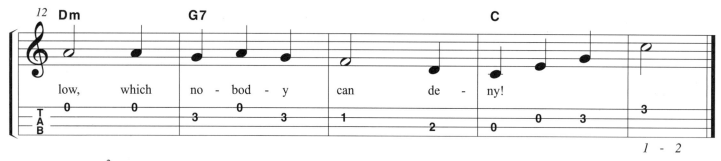

low, which no - bod - y can de - ny!

1 - 2

Legato is an Italian term that means to play smooth and connected with no separation between notes.

The ukulele has often been featured in popular music:
* *Two members of The Beatles, Paul McCartney and George Harrison, are both respected ukulele performers.*
* *Eddie Vedder of the rock group Pearl Jam recorded an album in 2011 album titled "Ukulele Songs."*
* *"Hey, Soul Sister" recorded by Train, is a very popular ukulele song to play and sing.*
* *Jake Shimabukuro recorded an excellent ukulele version of "While My Guitar Gently Weeps."*

14

TIES

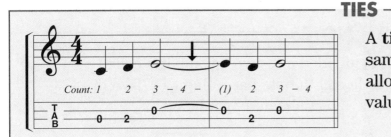

A **tie** connects two notes that are on the same line or space. Play the *first note only*, allowing it to sound for the combined value of both notes.

(14) Loose Ends

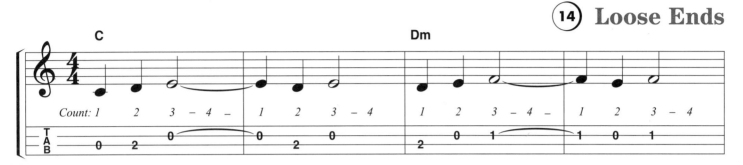

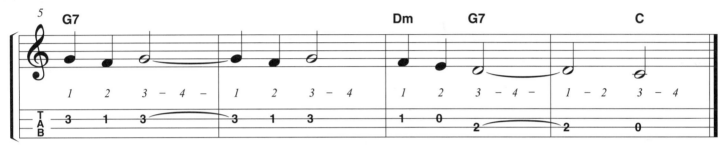

(15) When the Saints Go Marching In

Traditional

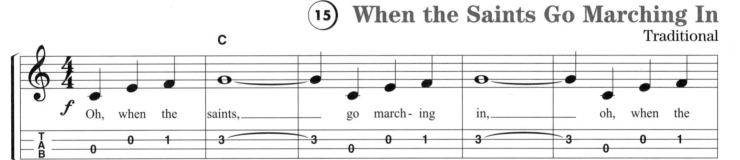

Oh, when the saints, go march-ing in, oh, when the

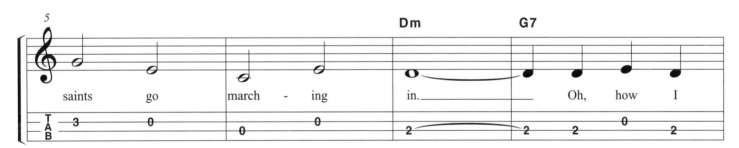

saints go march-ing in. Oh, how I

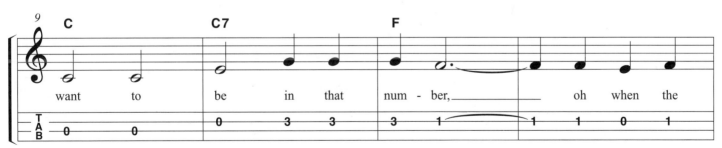

want to be in that num-ber, oh when the

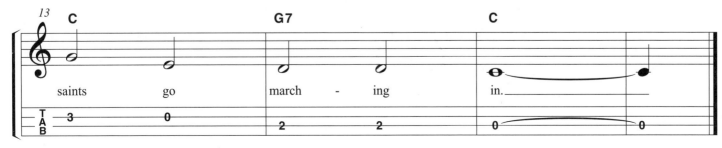

saints go march-ing in.

G1049

EIGHTH NOTES

A quarter note can be divided into two equal parts called **eighth notes**. A single eighth note has a **flag** (♪). Two or more eighth notes may be connected by a **beam** (♫).

♪ = ½ beat ♫ = 1 beat ♫♫ = 2 beats

Be sure you play eighth notes very smoothly and evenly.
Count: 1 + (and) 2 + 3 + 4 + as you play.

Study in Eighth Notes

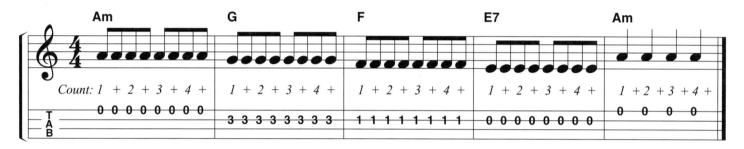

Playing eighth notes evenly is very important!

Picture This! 16

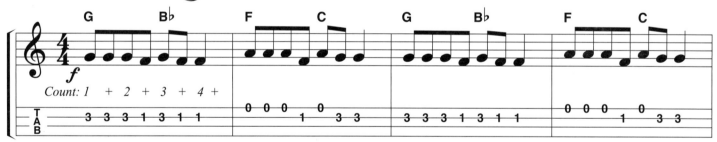

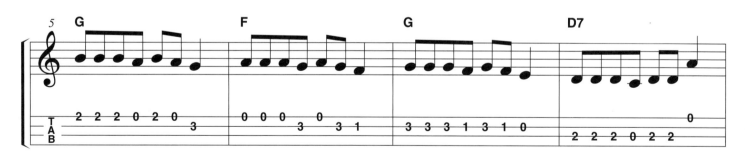

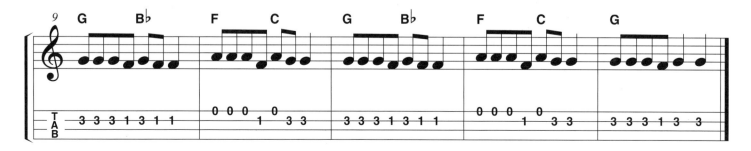

16

G1049

(17) See the Pony Run

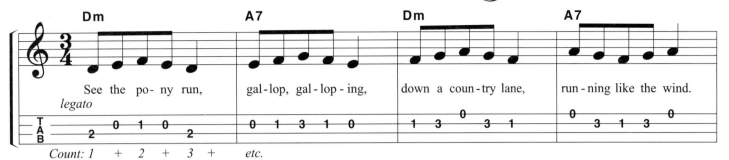

See the po-ny run, *legato* | gal-lop, gal-lop-ing, | down a coun-try lane, | run-ning like the wind.

Count: 1 + 2 + 3 + etc.

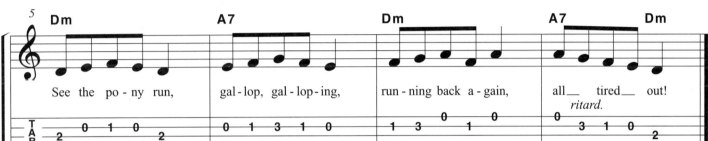

See the po-ny run, | gal-lop, gal-lop-ing, | run-ning back a-gain, | all tired out! *ritard.*

ritard. means to gradually get slower

You will occasionally see two or more note heads on one stem. Don't be alarmed, it is just a chord. Usually you will play chords by looking at a chord chart such as on page 30.

"Hands-on Hanon" ends with a C chord. Glide your thumb over the strings in a downward motion starting with the 4th string.

Ukulele Mike Sez:

"Use *Hands-on Hanon* as a daily warm-up piece to develop your technique."

(18) Hands-on Hanon

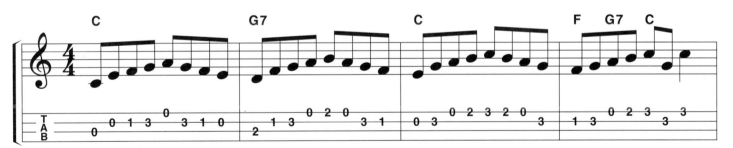

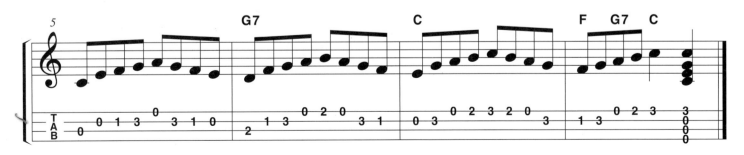

The Can Can (19)
Jacques Offenbach

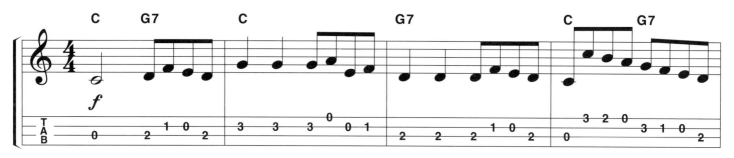

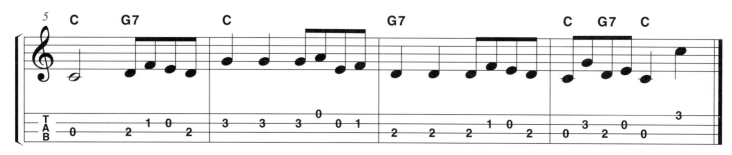

Michael Finnegan (20)
Traditional

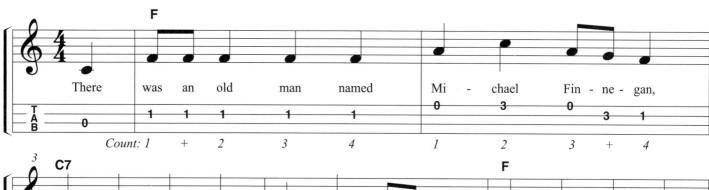

There was an old man named Mi - chael Fin - ne - gan,

Count: 1 + 2 3 4 1 2 3 + 4

he had whisk - ers on his chin - ne - gan. They fell out and

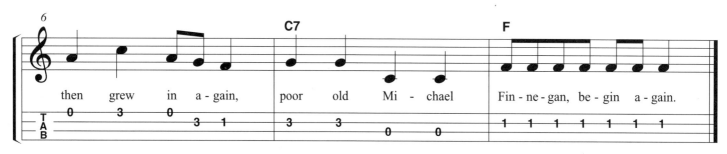

then grew in a - gain, poor old Mi - chael Fin - ne - gan, be - gin a - gain.

Be sure to keep a steady beat when playing eighth notes.

Key of A minor The key of A minor is relative to C major, meaning there are no sharps or flats in the **key signature** (page 32), and the melody centers around the note A, not C. The first and last chords of a song in the key of Am will probably be Am.

21 Rainy Day Ukulele

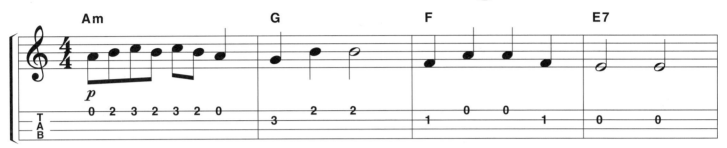

22 Jingle Bells

James Pierpont

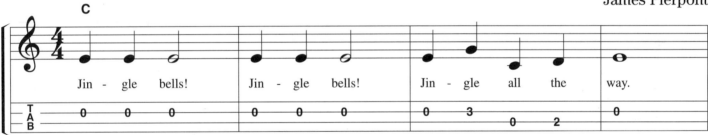

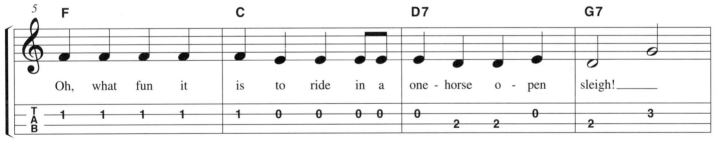

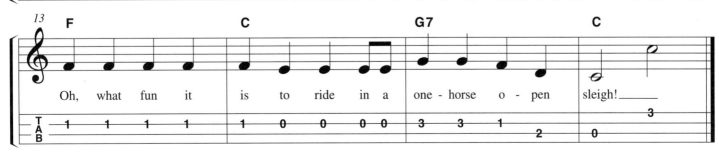

G1049

19

SHARPS

A **sharp** (♯) *raises* the pitch of a note by one fret (**one half step**).
The sharp symbol stays in effect until the end of a measure.

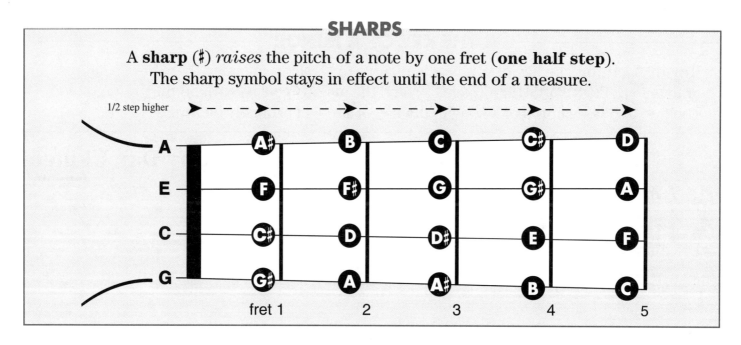

Sharp Warm-up (*Numbers placed above the note head indicate the left-hand fingering.*)

REPEAT SIGNS

Music enclosed by **repeat signs** is to be played again.

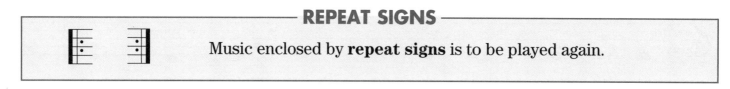

Obwisana (23)
Ghanaian

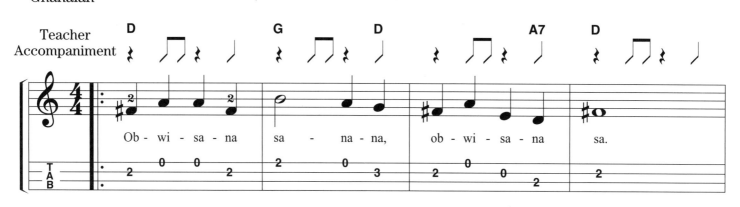

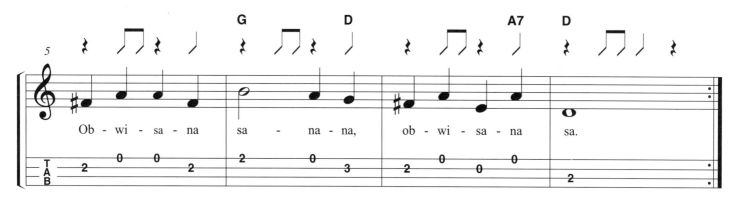

G1049

NATURALS

A **natural** (♮) *cancels* a sharp or a flat (page 24) previously used.

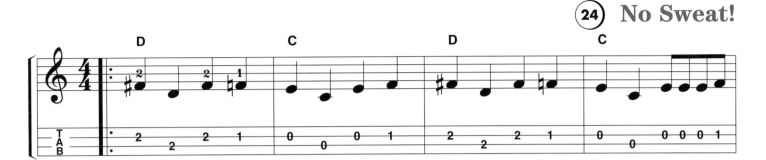

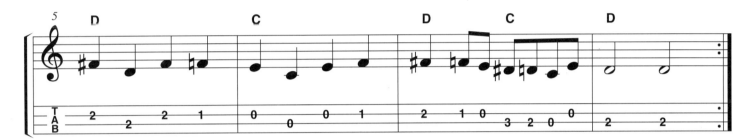

Speed Study *(Start slowly and evenly at first. Then gradually increase the tempo.)*

(25) **Medieval Nights**

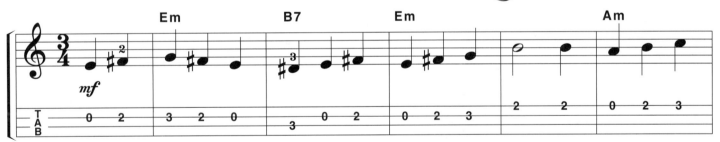

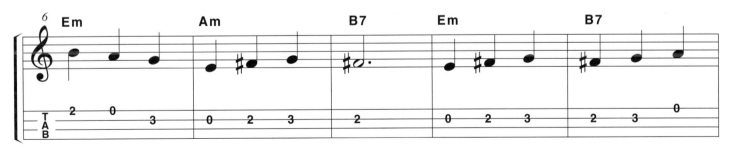

G1049

NOTES ON THE FOURTH STRING

open
string

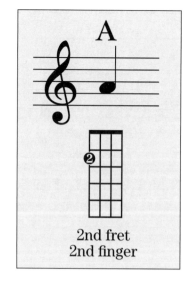

2nd fret
2nd finger

The two new notes on the fourth string can be played in other places. Follow the tablature to be sure you are playing the correct notes at the correct location. On page 38, you will learn more about a characteristic sound of the ukulele, referred to as **re-entrant tuning**. The fourth string is a very important component of this ukulele sound.

Study on G and A

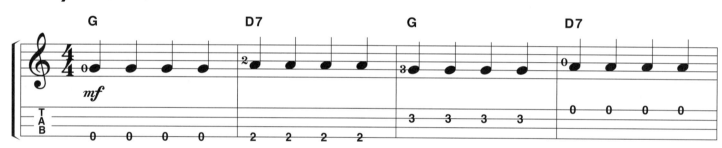

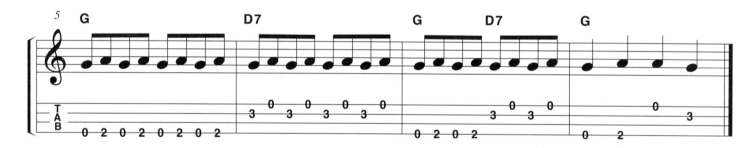

The two new notes above, G and A, will often times be played in two different locations, perhaps even in the same song. As you progress throughout this book, you will find that this feature of the ukulele provides a very pleasant, ringing sound.

Ukulele Mike Sez:
"Feel free to experiment with these two notes, playing them in different places."

G1049

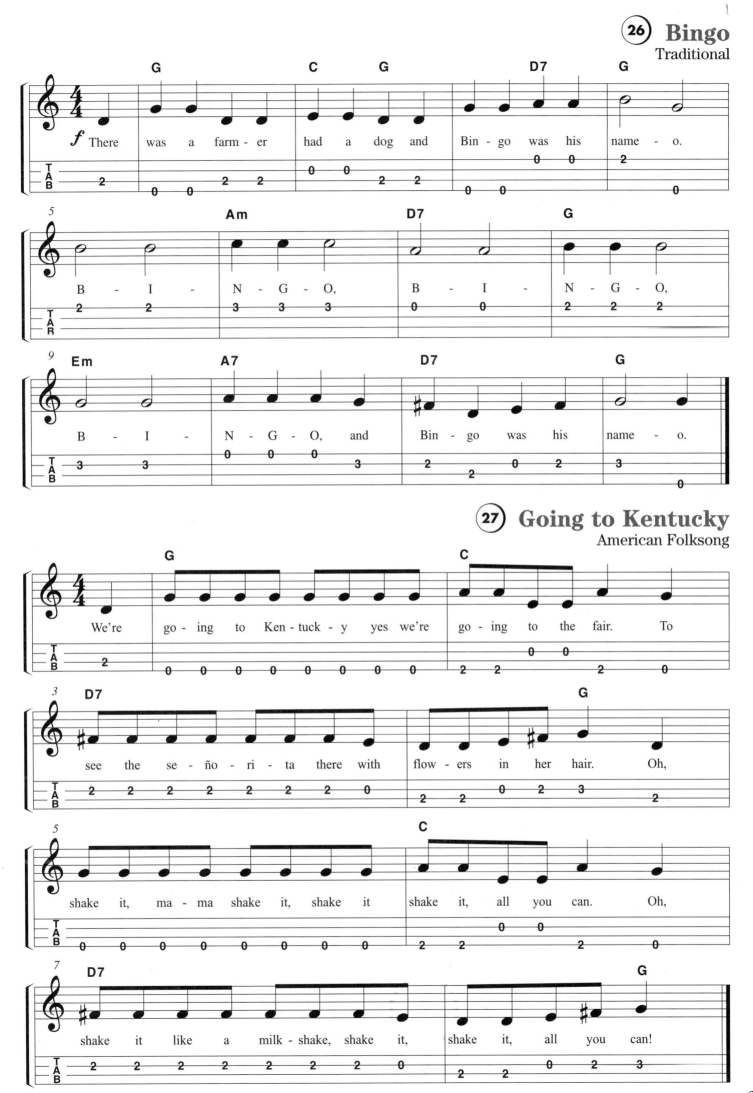

27 **Going to Kentucky**
American Folksong

A **flat** (♭) *lowers* the pitch of a note by one fret (one half step). The flat symbol stays in effect until the end of the measure. The chart below shows the location of flats, up to the fifth fret.

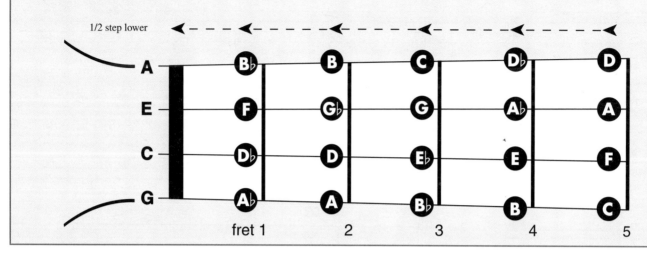

Flat Warm-up

The Streets of Laredo (28)
Traditional Cowboy Song

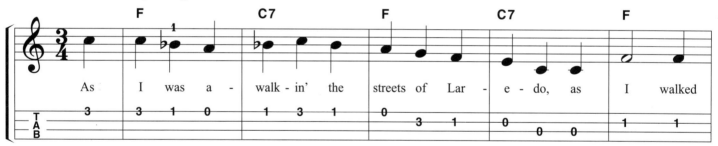

As I was a - walk - in' the streets of Lar - e - do, as I walked

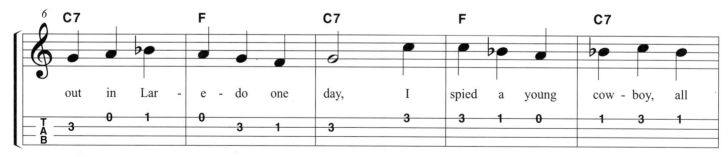

out in Lar - e - do one day, I spied a young cow - boy, all

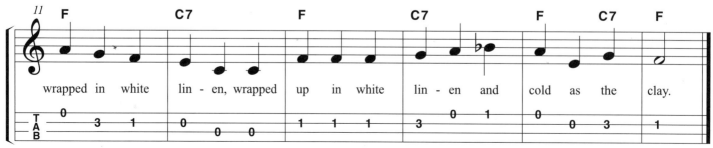

wrapped in white lin - en, wrapped up in white lin - en and cold as the clay.

24

DOTTED QUARTER NOTES

The **dotted quarter note** gets one and one half beats. ♩. = 1½ beats
The note following a dotted quarter note will often be an eighth note (♪).

Study in Dotted Quarter Notes *(Measures 1 and 2 should sound exactly the same!)*

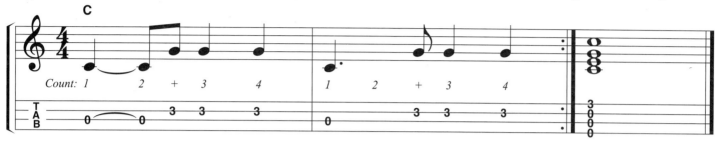

Count: 1   2   +   3   4   1   2   +   3   4

(29) *Alouette*

French-Canadian Folksong

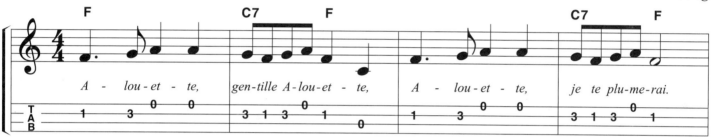

A - lou-et - te,   gen-tille A-lou-et - te,   A - lou-et - te,   je te plu-me-rai.

Je te plu-me-rai la tête,   je te plu-me-rai la tête.   Et la tête,   et la tête.

Et la tête,   et la tête.   Oh,_____   A - lou - et - te,

gen-tille A-lou-et - te,   A - lou-et - te,   je te plu-me-rai.

ENHARMONIC NOTES

Notes that have the same pitch, but different names, are called **enharmonic notes**.
One of the notes will be a sharp note; the other will be a flat note; for example, F♯ and G♭.
Write in the missing enharmonic notes. **Hint**: The letter names will be in alphabetical order.

D♯ and _____♭   _____♯ and D♭   A♯ and _____♭   _____♯ and A♭

NEW NOTES ON THE FIRST STRING

Below are notes on the first string up to the seventh fret. Pairs of notes in brackets are **enharmonic notes**, notes that are played in the same place but with different names.

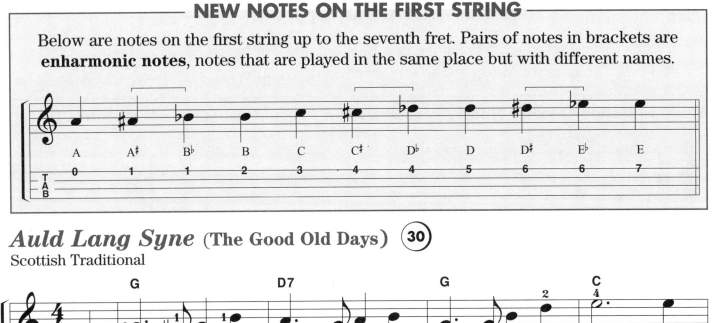

Auld Lang Syne (The Good Old Days) 30
Scottish Traditional

Should auld ac- quaint-ance be for-got and nev - er brought to mind? Should

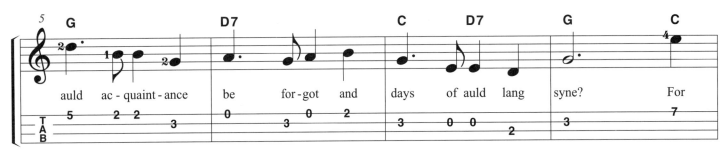

auld ac - quaint-ance be for-got and days of auld lang syne? For

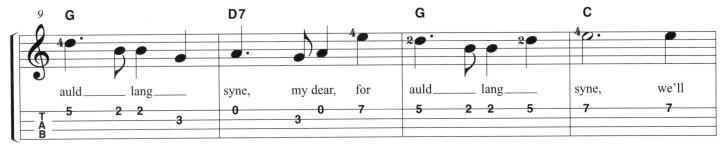

auld____ lang____ syne, my dear, for auld____ lang____ syne, we'll

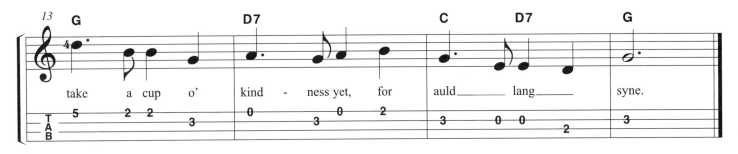

take a cup o' kind - ness yet, for auld____ lang____ syne.

Hint: Since there are not any notes on the first fret in this song, keep your first finger on the 2nd fret and your 2nd finger on the 3rd fret. This will make it easier to reach the 7th fret.

Numbers placed either next to or above the note head are indications for left-hand fingering. Follow these indications in order to make the movement of the left hand as smooth as possible.

G1049

Duet A duet is a piece of music for two performers. The ability to play well with others is one of the top requirements of a good musician. Learn to play Part I and Part II.

(31) *Dona Nobis Pacem*
(Give Us Peace)
Anonymous

STUDENT DUET

Preparation for Barre Chords

Some chords require one finger to play two or more strings at the same time. This technique is referred to as a **barre chord**. Keep your first finger straight and press firmly so that all of the strings are sounding clearly. In the exercise below, notice that the third string open is in each chord. The tablature will help you to learn this rock-sounding song quickly.

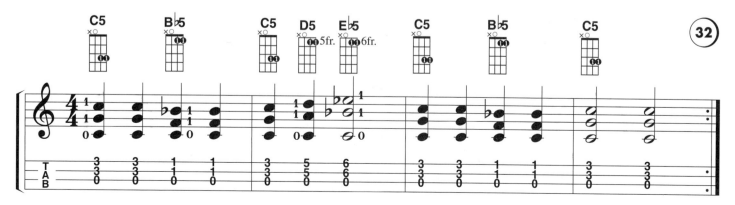

HAMMER-ON

Two or more different notes may be connected by a curved line called a **slur**. When the second note is a higher pitch than the first, use a **hammer-on**. Play the first note with your thumb, then let the left-hand finger drop (like a hammer) to sound the second note.

Hammer-on Warm-up (33)

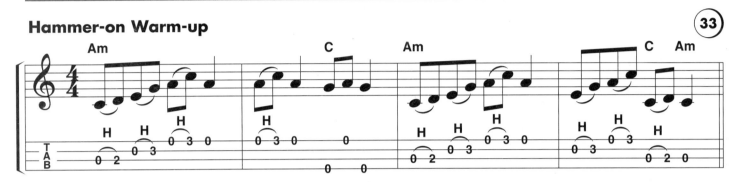

PULL-OFF

A **pull-off** is a slur in which the second note is a *lower* pitch than the first (the opposite of a hammer-on). Play the first note with your thumb, then *pull* your left-hand finger *off* (toward the floor) to sound the second note.

Pull-off Warm-up (34)

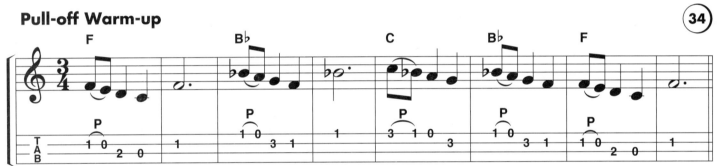

Ukulele Mike Sez:
"Begin by concentrating on playing the right notes at the right time. *Then* add the hammer-ons and pull-offs. If these techniques are a little too difficult for now, come back to them later."

Blues Riffin' (35)

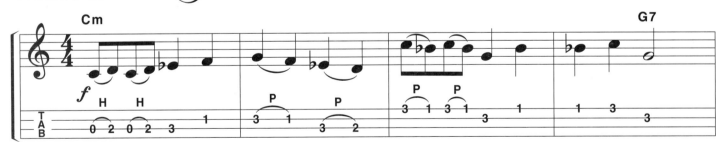

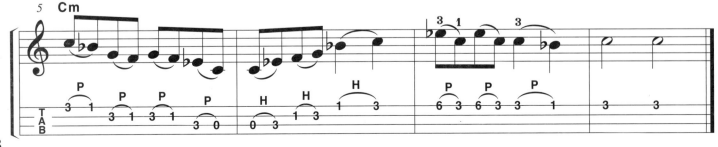

G1049

RESTS

A **rest** is a moment of *silence* in music. Each note value has an equal rest value.

whole	*half*	*quarter*	*eighth*
𝗼 ▬ = 4 beats	♩ ▬ = 2 beats	♩ 𝄽 = 1 beat	♪ ꞌ = ½ beat

Uke tip

__Dampen__ the strings when necessary. Release the pressure of a left-hand finger to stop a string from vibrating. To dampen an open string, use the fingers of the left hand to lightly touch the vibrating strings.

36 Sleep Walk

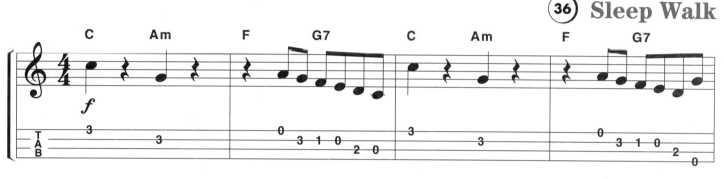

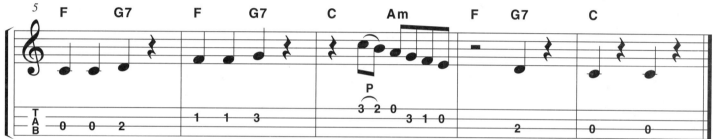

37 America

Words by Samuel F. Smith
Music: *Thesaurus Musicus*

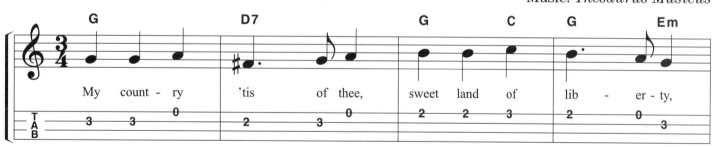

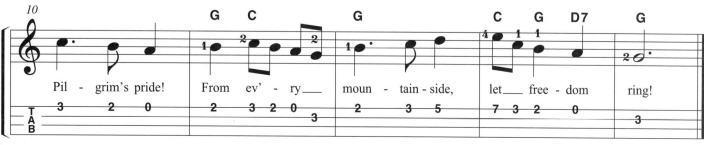

G1049

CHORDS

Chords are fun and easy to learn. Below are several chords that are grouped together in popular ukulele keys. Every key has three chords that are used often. They are called the **primary chords.**

Follow these two easy steps to learn how to strum chords:
1) Memorize the fingering for each chord, be sure that every string sounds clearly.
2) Use your right-hand thumb to strum a steady beat (pulse), don't speed up or slow down.

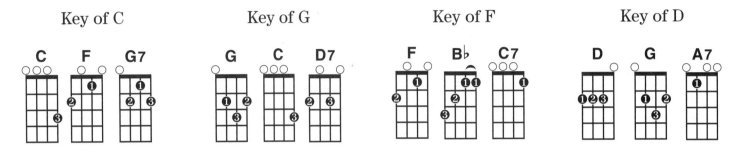

Right-Hand Strum

Thumb Stroke Gently brush down across all four strings. Use a steady pulse, strumming on each beat. Refer to track 38. This strum will sound well with any song in $\frac{4}{4}$ time.

A slash mark (/) indicates a quarter-note strum.

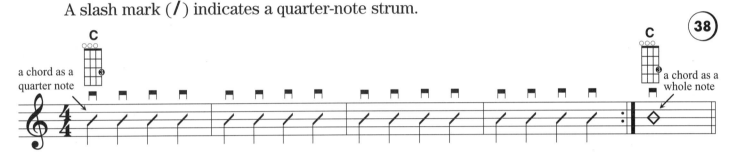

Ukulele Mike Sez:
"Strum evenly without any gaps between the chord changes. Don't strum too fast."

Now strum while changing chords. Strum slowly and be sure to keep a steady beat, especially when changing chords. The chords that follow are the primary chords in the key of C.

Key of C

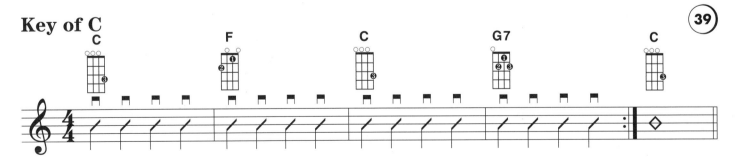

Whenever possible, learn both the melody and the chords to a song. Strum with a steady beat, especially when changing from one chord to another. Go back to the beginning of the book and strum the chords to as many of the songs as you can. Strumming chords on the ukulele is most enjoyable, especially if you or someone else can sing the lyrics to the songs! See pages 46 and 47 for more chords and strums.

Now strum the primary chords in the keys of G, F, and D.

Key of G

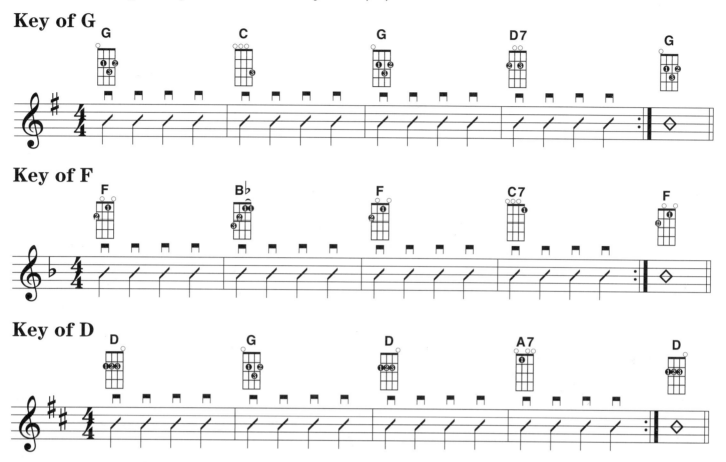

Key of F

Key of D

The first time you play "Arpeggio Study," strum the chords using quarter notes. On the repeat, play the melody, which uses a musical technique called an **arpeggio**.

An arpeggio is playing the notes of a chord one string at a time, instead of strumming all the strings together.

⑩ Arpeggio Study

Let ring When playing the melody, allow the strings to vibrate as long as possible.

Notice the sharp (♯) placed on the F line after the G clef. This is the **key signature** for the Key of G. A song in the key of G will have *all* the F notes played as sharps. Songs that use the notes in the G scale are said to be in the **Key of G**. The first and last chords in the song will probably be G.

Notes of the G major scale

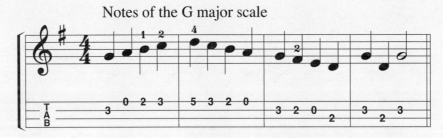

The Birthday Song (41)
Traditional Melody

Ukulele Mike Sez:
"Strum with an even pulse. Don't try to match the rhythm of the melody."

🎵 = *fermata*, hold the note longer than usual

Goodnight Ladies (42)
Traditional

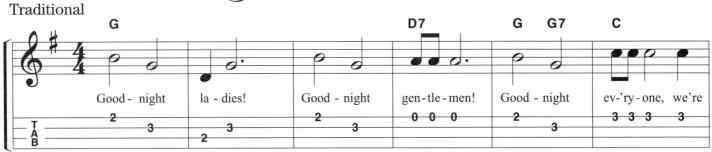

Good - night la - dies! Good - night gen - tle - men! Good - night ev - 'ry - one, we're

go - ing to leave you now. Mer - ri - ly we roll a - long, roll a - long,

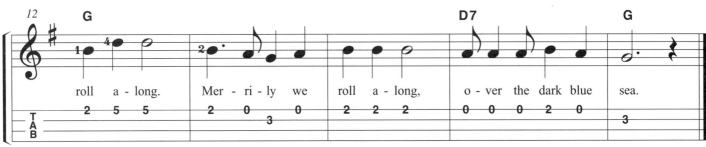

roll a - long. Mer - ri - ly we roll a - long, o - ver the dark blue sea.

G1049

COMMON CHORDS IN THE KEY OF G MAJOR (Em)

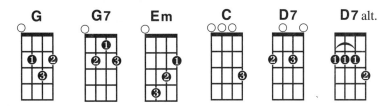

Key of E minor The key of E minor is relative to G major, meaning that all of the F notes are still sharp, but the melody centers around the note E, not G. The key signature is the same as the key of G major. The first and last chords of the song will probably be Em.

43 The Snake Charmer
Traditional

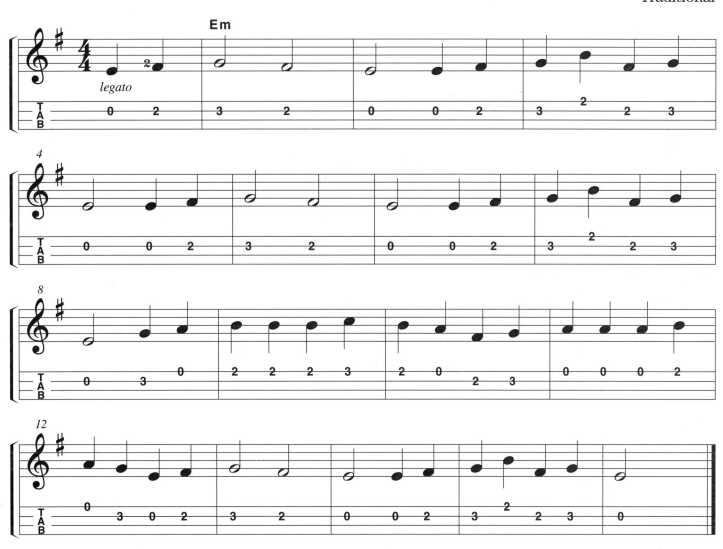

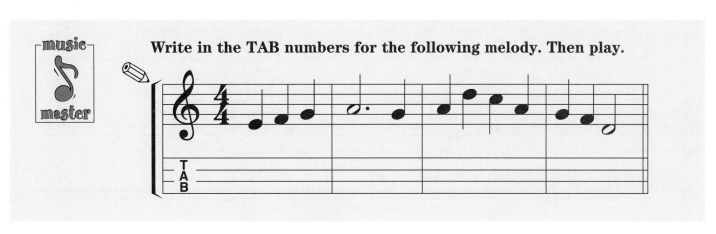

Write in the TAB numbers for the following melody. Then play.

THE KEY OF F MAJOR

A song in the key of F will have *all* the B notes played as flats. Notice the new key signature. Songs that use the notes in the F scale are said to be in the **Key of F**. The first and last chords will probably be F.

Notes of the F major scale

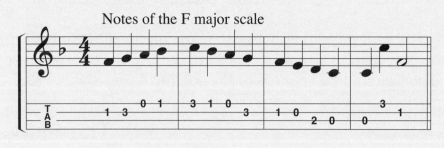

Skipping Stones (44)

Eighth-Note Strum - use down and up strokes as indicated. See page 47.

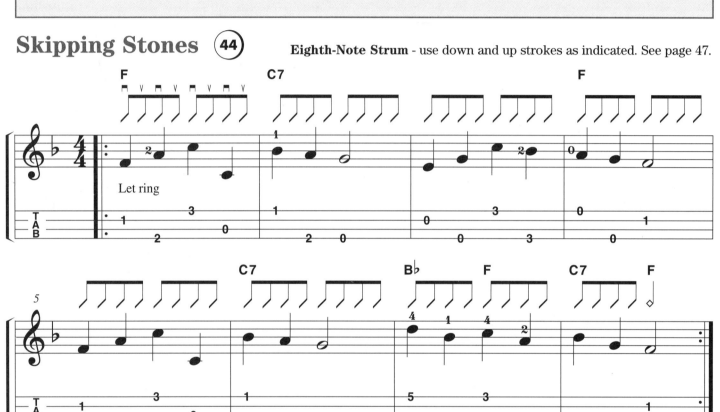

A Maiden Faire (45)

34

G1049

COMMON CHORDS IN THE KEY OF F MAJOR (Dm)

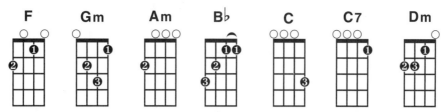

Key of D minor The key of D minor is relative to F major, meaning that all of the B notes are still flat, but the melody centers around the note D, not F. The key signature is the same as the key of F major. The first and last chords will probably be Dm.

46 Hymn

*When strumming chords on the ukulele, you will often be playing the same note on two different strings. This is referred to as **unison**. See measure 2 in "Taking a Morning Walk."*

47 Taking a Morning Walk

THE KEY OF D MAJOR

The **key signature** for the Key of D is F♯ and C♯.

All F and C notes will be played sharp.

Notes of the D major scale

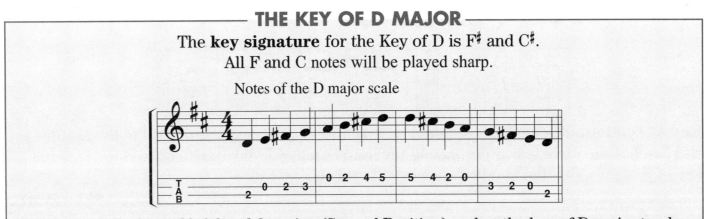

Following the indicated left-hand fingering (Second Position) makes the key of D easier to play.

Ukulele Mike Sez:

"You will be playing *Tingalayo* in Second Position. Play all key of D songs in **Second Position.** See page 48."

Tingalayo (48)

Traditional

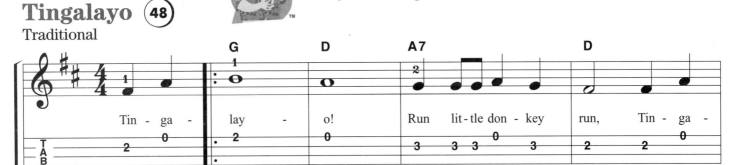

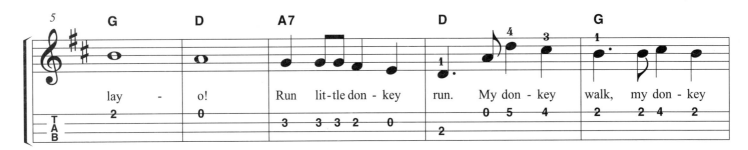

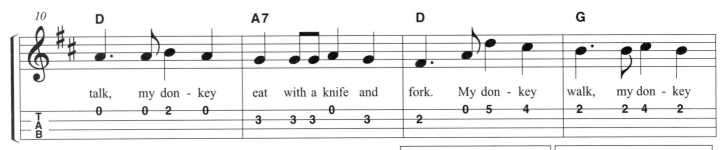

1ST AND 2ND ENDINGS

Play the first ending and take the repeat.

Then play the second ending, skipping over the first ending.

36

G1049

COMMON CHORDS IN THE KEY OF D MAJOR (Bm)

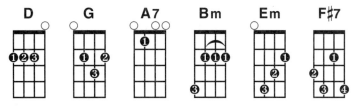

Key of B minor The key of B minor is the relative minor of D major.

(49) **Joy To the World**

Words by Isaac Watts
Music arranged by Lowell Mason

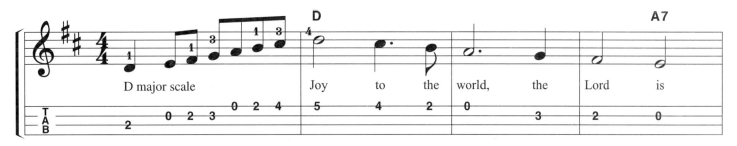

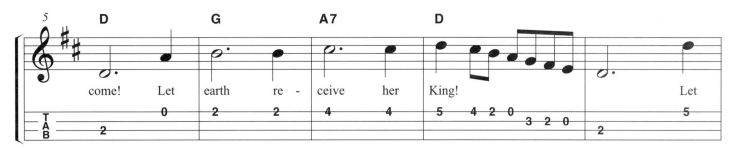

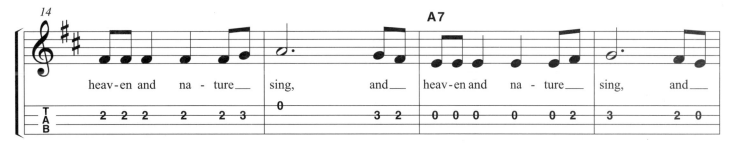

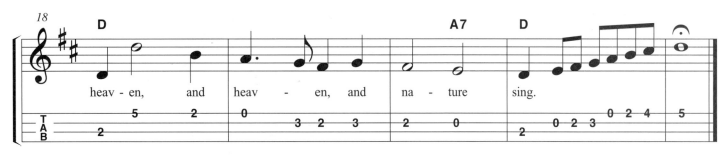

RE-ENTRANT TUNING

Re-entrant tuning means that the strings of the ukulele don't run from low to high in pitch as you move through the strings, for example as they do as on a guitar. On the ukulele, this brings out an extra sparkle to your performance, a trademark sound of the ukulele. The **Let ring** technique is a very important part of this ukulele feature along with playing G on the open 4th string rather than on the 2nd string, third fret.

Ukulele Mike Sez:
"Be sure to look at the key signature before you start playing."

Hush Little Baby 50
Traditional

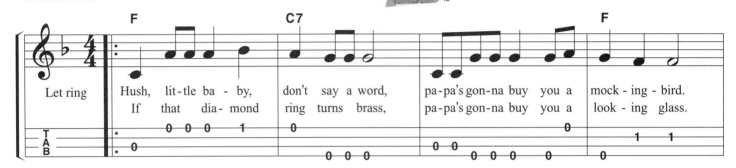

Additional Lyrics

If that billy goat don't pull, Papa's gonna buy you a cart and bull.
If that cart and bull turn over, Papa's gonna buy you a dog named Rover.
If that dog named Rover won't bark. Papa's gonna to buy you a horse and cart.
If that horse and cart fall down, you'll still be the sweetest little baby in town.

Ukulele March 51

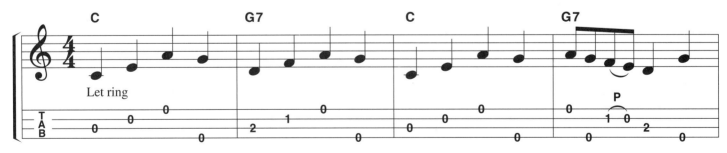

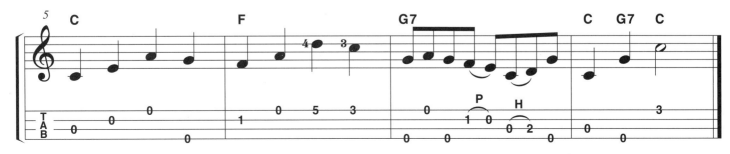

52 What Can You Do with a Ukulele?

Sea Shanty Melody

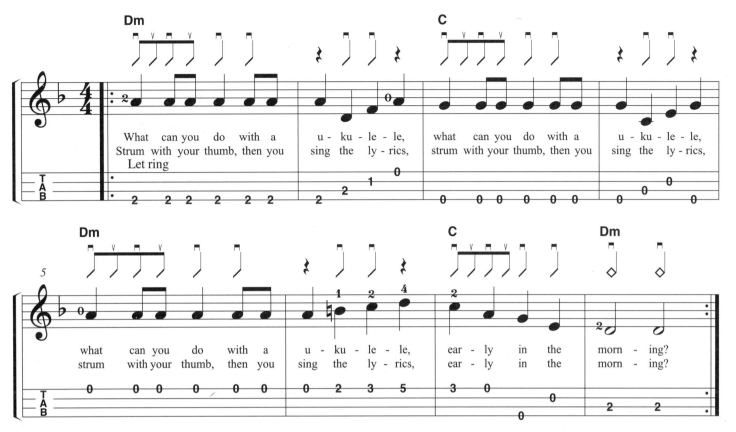

Additional Lyrics
Play it so soft, and then get louder, early in the morning.
Play it so fast, or play it slower, early in the morning.

Most of the songs you have already learned will sound good using G on the open 4th string rather than the 2nd string, 3rd fret. The following songs work exceptionally well, but there are many others you will enjoy.

By the Sea page 10   *Sail Away* page 12
Pop! Goes the Weasel! page 13   *See the Pony Run* page 17
Alouette page 25   *America* page 29

53 Rolling With the Waves

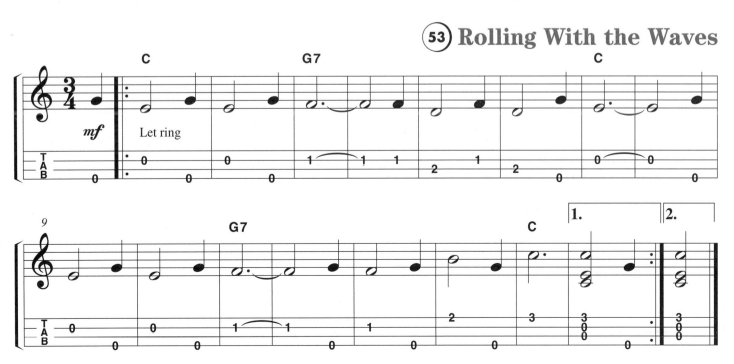

CHORD REVIEW CHART
for pages 40–41

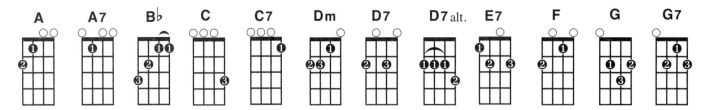

The Yellow Rose of Texas
Traditional

54

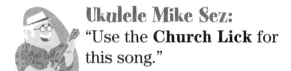

Ukulele Mike Sez: "Use the **Church Lick** for this song."

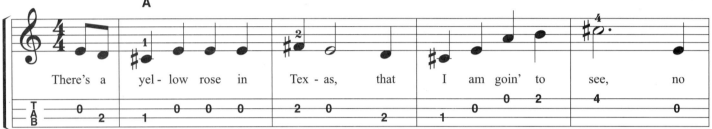

There's a yel - low rose in Tex - as, that I am goin' to see, no

oth - er fel - low knows her, no fel - low on - ly me. She___

cried so when I left her, it like to break my heart, and

if I ev - er find her, we nev - er - more will part.

Aloha Oe (Farewell to Thee) 55
Queen Lili'uokalani

Featured in the 2005 movie *Lilo & Stitch 2: Island Favorites*!

Fare - well to thee, fare - well to thee, thou charm - ing one who

G1049

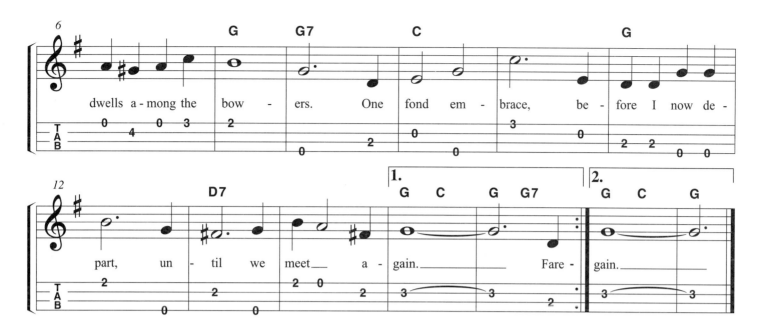

(56) **Good King Wenceslas**

Traditional

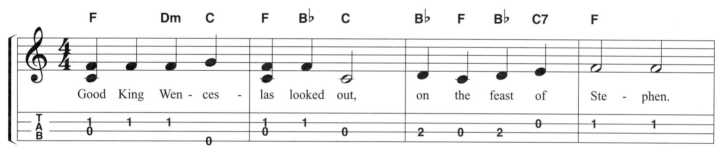

Good King Wen-ces-las looked out, on the feast of Ste - phen.

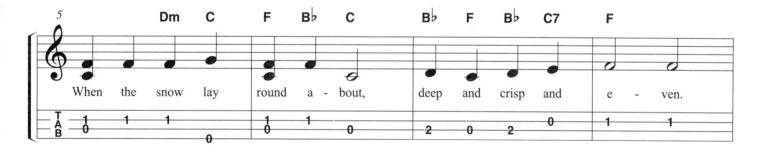

When the snow lay round a - bout, deep and crisp and e - ven.

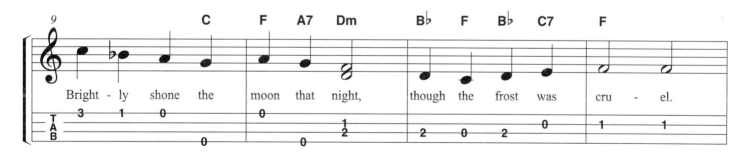

Bright - ly shone the moon that night, though the frost was cru - el.

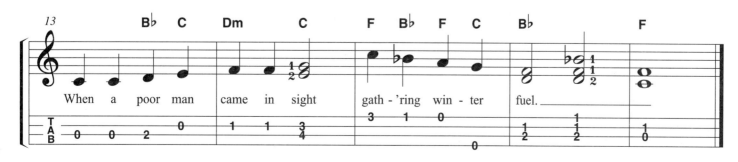

When a poor man came in sight gath-'ring win - ter fuel.

NEW NOTES ON THE SECOND AND THIRD STRINGS

Below are higher notes on the second and third strings, up to the fifth fret. The pairs of notes in brackets are **enharmonic notes**, notes that are played in the same place but with different names.

Just for Fun 57

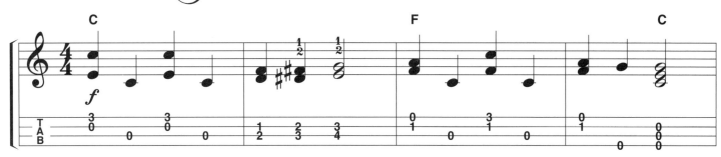

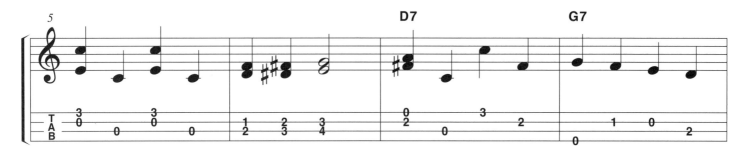

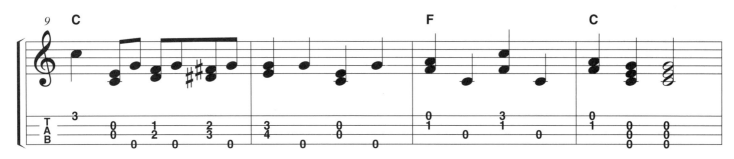

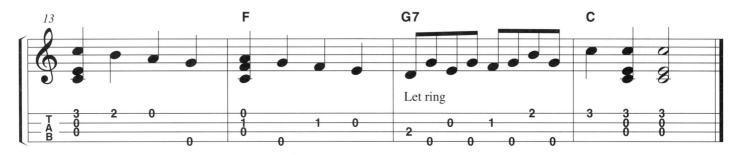

Ukulele Mike Sez:
"Use your thumb to play one, two, three, or even four notes in the melody."

G1049

Uke tip

"*A Seafaring Tale*" *uses many new techniques that you have learned as well as several new chords. Once you have learned to play the correct notes at the correct time, be sure to follow all of the indicated techniques: dynamics, Let ring, hammer-on, pull-off, and ritard.*

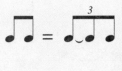

Swing rhythm (sometimes referred to as a **shuffle**), is a musical style that uses an uneven eighth-note rhythm with long and short values. Based on triplets by tying the first two notes of the group, swing gives the melody a pleasing jazz sound. The downbeats (beats 1, 2, 3, and 4) will always be long; the upbeats (the "and" or "+" of the beat) will always be short. Swing rhythm is indicated at the beginning of the music.

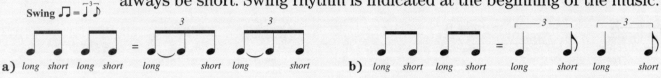

Swing Warm-up (*Count: long - short along with track 59 to "feel" the swing rhythm.*)

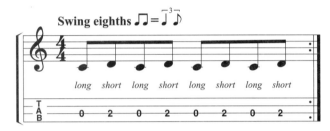

Ukulele Mike Sez:
"Listen to the audio tracks often to get the feel of swing rhythm."

The "C" Street Rag (59)

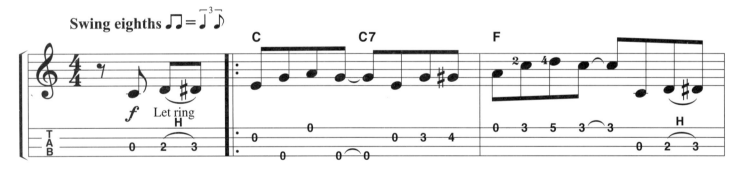

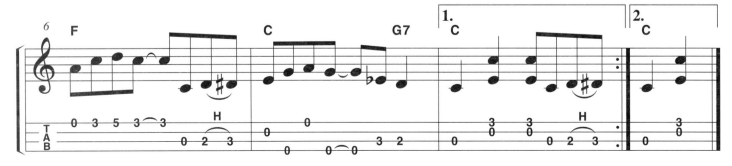

A **slide** is a technique where you pick the first note with your right hand and then slide to the next note (target note) without picking the string a second time. You will need to press firmly so the 2nd note can be heard clearly.

Slide Warm-up

60 **Saint Louis Blues**

William C. Handy

G1049

COMMON UKULELE CHORDS

- These chords are arranged in alphabetical order, making it easy to find a desired chord quickly.

- Left-hand fingerings were chosen for ease of play, and voicings were chosen for their pleasing sound.

- Students are encouraged to learn as many chords as possible.

- Diminished sevenths chords are very interesting chords. Any note of the chord can be considered the root note. There are only four diminished seventh chords, and each one has four different names: 1) C#dim7, Edim7, Gdim7, B♭dim7; 2) Ddim7, Fdim7, A♭dim7, Bdim7; 3) E♭dim7, G♭dim7, Adim7, Cdim7; 4) Edim7, Gdim7, B♭dim7, C#dim7.

- You will find that there are some chords that have different names but are played the same way, such as C6 and Am7.

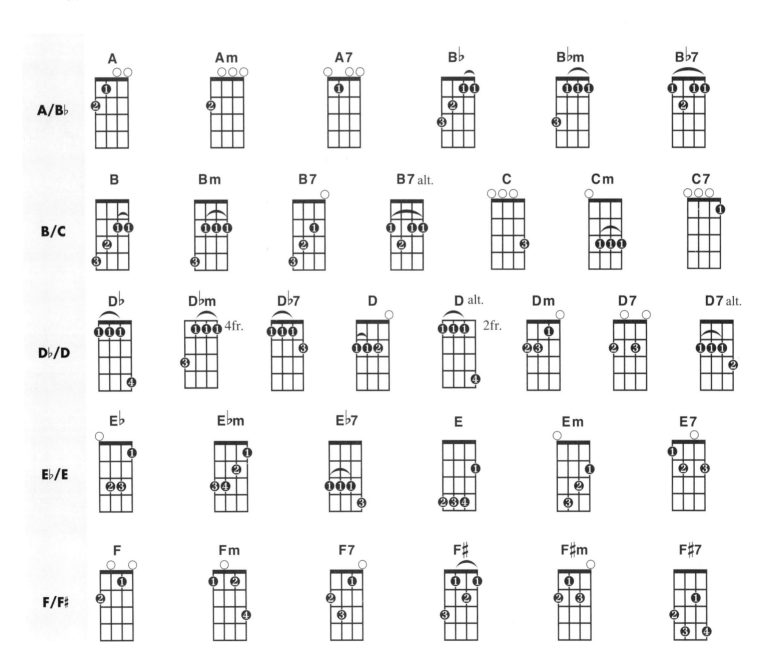

46

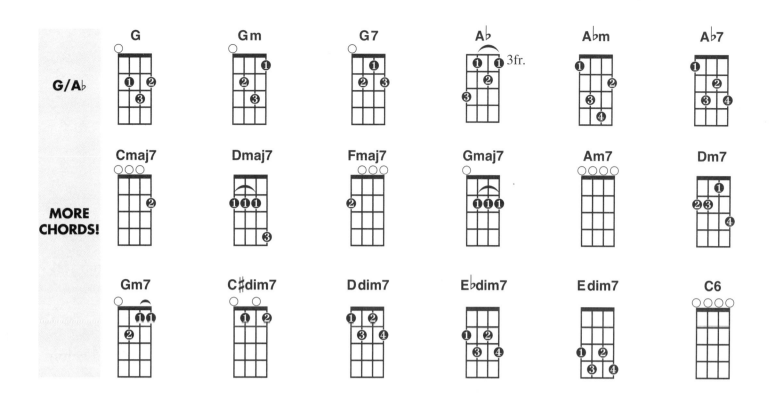

STRUMMING PATTERNS

Here are strumming patterns that you will really enjoy. Use your thumb or the nail of your index finger for the down stroke (⊓) and then use the flesh of the index finger for the up stroke (∨). Listen to track 61 to hear these strums.

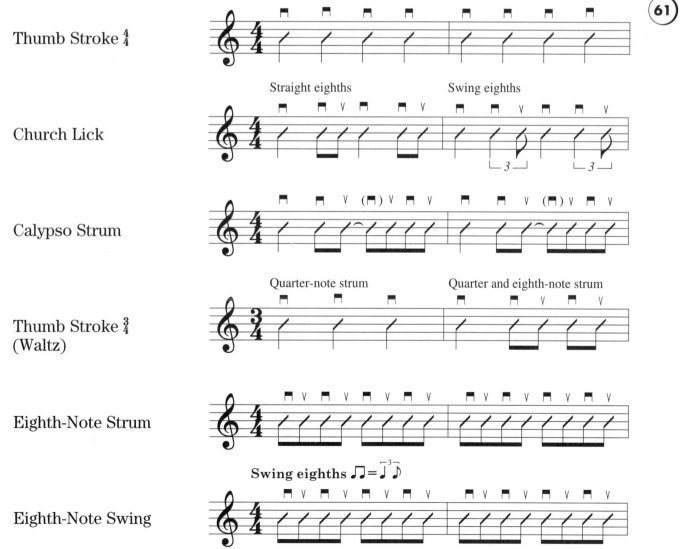

GLOSSARY

SIGN	TERM	DEFINITION
	arpeggio	The notes of a chord played one after the other, instead of at the same time. (pg. 31)
	chord	Three or more notes played at the same time. (pg. 30)
	dampening	Using the left or right hand to stop the strings from sounding. (pg. 29)
	enharmonic notes	Notes that are played in the same place but have different names. (C♯ - D♭, D♯ - E♭, F♯ - G♭, G♯ - A♭, A♯ - B♭). (pg. 42)
⌢	**fermata**	Indicates that a note or a rest should be held longer than usual. (pg. 32)
♭	**flat**	Lowers the pitch of a note by one fret (one half step). (pg. 24)
	key signature	The sharps or flats at the beginning of each line of music which indicate the key of the music. (pg. 32)
	legato	Play smoothly. (pg. 14)
	Let ring	Allow the strings to vibrate as long as possible. (pg. 31)
	major scale	A series of pitches arranged in ascending or descending order. (pg. 11)
♮	**natural**	Cancels a sharp or flat used earlier. (pg. 21)
▬ ▬ 𝄽 𝄾	**rests**	Indicate a moment of silence in music. (pg. 29)
	ritard.	Gradually becoming slower. (pg. 17)
	Second Position	Left-hand finger: 1 plays notes on the 2nd fret. 2 plays notes on the 3rd fret. 3 plays notes on the 4th fret. 4 plays notes on the 5th fret. (pg. 36)
♯	**sharp**	Raises the pitch of a note by one fret (one half step.) (pg. 20)
	steps	Notes that are one letter name apart, moving in *line-space* or *space-line* order. A half step is the distance of one fret. A whole step is the distance of two frets. (pg. 20)

NATURAL NOTES ON THE UKULELE

G1049